COOKING 101

VERY SIMPLE RECIPES FOR DELICIOUS BASIC COOKING

By
BookSumo Press
Copyright © by Saxonberg Associates

Published by
BookSumo Press, a DBA of Saxonberg Associates
http://www.booksumo.com/

ABOUT THE AUTHOR.

BookSumo Press is a publisher of unique, easy, and healthy cookbooks.

Our cookbooks span all topics and all subjects. If you want a deep dive into the possibilities of cooking with any type of ingredient. Then BookSumo Press is your go to place for robust yet simple and delicious cookbooks and recipes. Whether you are looking for great tasting pressure cooker recipes or authentic ethic and cultural food. BookSumo Press has a delicious and easy cookbook for you.

With simple ingredients, and even simpler step-by-step instructions BookSumo cookbooks get everyone in the kitchen chefing delicious meals.

BookSumo is an independent publisher of books operating in the beautiful Garden State (NJ) and our team of chefs and kitchen experts are here to teach, eat, and be merry!

INTRODUCTION

Welcome to *The Effortless Chef Series*! Thank you for taking the time to purchase this cookbook.

Come take a journey into the delights of easy cooking. The point of this cookbook and all BookSumo Press cookbooks is to exemplify the effortless nature of cooking simply.

In this book we focus on simple cooking. You will find that even though the recipes are simple, the taste of the dishes are quite amazing.

So will you take an adventure in simple cooking? If the answer is yes please consult the table of contents to find the dishes you are most interested in.

Once you are ready, jump right in and start cooking.

— BookSumo Press

TABLE OF CONTENTS

ANY ISSUES? CONTACT US

If you find that something important to you is missing from this book please contact us at info@booksumo.com.

We will take your concerns into consideration when the 2nd edition of this book is published. And we will keep you updated!

— BookSumo Press

LEGAL NOTES

COMMON ABBREVIATIONS

cup(s)	C.
tablespoon	tbsp
teaspoon	tsp
ounce	oz.
pound	lb

*All units used are standard American measurements

CHAPTER 1: EASY SIMPLE RECIPES

EGGS IN A BOAT

Ingredients

- 1/2 tbsp butter
- 1 slice white bread
- 1 egg

Directions

- Coat your bread with butter on each of its sides. Then cut-out a circle in the middle of it.
- Whisk your egg in a small bowl. Set it aside.
- Get a skillet hot and for 1 min fry each side of the bread. Pour the egg into the hole and cook for 3 more mins.
- Enjoy.

Amount per serving (1 total)

Timing Information:

Preparation	Cooking	Total Time
10 m	10 m	20 m

Nutritional Information:

Calories	189 kcal
Fat	11.6 g
Carbohydrates	13g
Protein	8.3 g
Cholesterol	201 mg
Sodium	281 mg

* Percent Daily Values are based on a 2,000 calorie diet.

TOMATO FETA EGGS

Ingredients

- 1 tbsp butter
- 1/4 cup chopped onion
- 4 eggs, beaten
- 1/4 cup chopped tomatoes
- 2 tbsps crumbled feta cheese
- salt and pepper to taste

Directions

- Fry onions until see-through, in butter, in a frying pan. Then mix in your eggs. While the eggs are frying make sure to stir them so that they become scrambled.
- Before the eggs are completely cooked add in your pepper and salt, then your feta, and finally your tomatoes.
- Continue to let the eggs fry until the feta melts.

Amount per serving (4 total)

Timing Information:

Preparation	Cooking	Total Time
10 m	5 m	15 m

Nutritional Information:

Calories	116 kcal
Fat	8.9 g
Carbohydrates	2g
Protein	7.2 g
Cholesterol	198 mg
Sodium	435 mg

* Percent Daily Values are based on a 2,000 calorie diet.

Eggs from France

Ingredients

- 1/2 cup butter
- 1/2 cup flour
- salt and pepper to taste
- 1 quart milk
- 8 slices white bread, toasted
- 8 hard-cooked eggs
- 1 pinch paprika

Directions

- First get a saucepan hot before doing anything else.
- Enter your butter into the saucepan and let it melt completely.
- Then add in your flour, stir it a bit, and let it cook for 10 mins until it becomes lighter in colour.
- Mix in your milk and wait until everything is lightly boiling, then set the heat to low.
- Let it cook for 10 more mins.

- Add in some pepper and salt.
- Remove the yolks from each egg. Then you want to dice the egg whites and mix them into the simmering sauce.
- Get a strainer and press the eggs through it. Put this in a bowl.
- Put half a cup of simmering sauce on a piece of toasted bread and garnish the bread with the yolks and some paprika.
- Enjoy.

Amount per serving (8 total)

Timing Information:

Preparation	Cooking	Total Time
10 m	20 m	30 m

Nutritional Information:

Calories	336 kcal
Fat	20.1 g
Carbohydrates	25g
Protein	13.2 g
Cholesterol	252 mg
Sodium	413 mg

* Percent Daily Values are based on a 2,000 calorie diet.

BURRITOS 101

Ingredients

- 1 (10 inch) flour tortilla
- 1/4 C. vegetarian refried beans
- 1 slice American cheese
- 1 pinch ground black pepper
- 1 tsp low-fat sour cream
- 1 dash hot pepper sauce

Directions

- For five mins warm your refried beans.
- Then warm your tortillas in the microwave for 30 secs.
- Layer beans into the tortilla then some sour cream then cheese, and some pepper.
- Finally add some hot sauce.
- Form everything into a burrito.
- Enjoy.

Amount per serving (1 total)

Timing Information:

Preparation	Cooking	Total Time
15 m	20 m	1 hr

Nutritional Information:

Calories	400 kcal
Fat	10 g
Carbohydrates	49.9g
Protein	15.8 g
Cholesterol	29 mg
Sodium	1075 mg

* Percent Daily Values are based on a 2,000 calorie diet.

Advanced Ramen

Ingredients

- 2 1/2 cups water
- 1 carrot, sliced
- 4 fresh mushrooms, sliced
- 1 (3 ounce) package ramen noodle pasta with flavor packet
- 1 egg, lightly beaten
- 1/4 cup milk (optional)

Directions

- Cook carrots and mushrooms in boiling water for about seven minutes before adding noodles and flavoring packets, and cooking all this for three more minutes.
- Pour egg into the mixture very slowly, while stirring continuously for thirty seconds to get the egg cooked.
- Add some milk before serving.

Serving: 1

Timing Information:

Preparation	Cooking	Total Time
5 mins	10 mins	15 mins

Nutritional Information:

Calories	500 kcal
Carbohydrates	66 g
Cholesterol	191 mg
Fat	19.2 g
Fiber	4.5 g
Protein	17.4 g
Sodium	1796 mg

* Percent Daily Values are based on a 2,000 calorie diet.

CHEESY RAMEN

Ingredients

- 2 cups water
- 1 (3 ounce) package any flavor ramen noodles
- 1 slice American cheese

Directions

- Cook ramen noodles in boiling water for about 2 minutes and drain it with a strainer before stirring in seasoning packet and cheese.
- Serve.

Serving: 1

Timing Information:

Preparation	Cooking	Total Time
5 mins		5 mins

Nutritional Information:

Calories	163 kcal
Carbohydrates	7.9 g
Cholesterol	27 mg
Fat	11.3 g
Fiber	0.4 g
Protein	7.5 g
Sodium	733 mg

* Percent Daily Values are based on a 2,000 calorie diet.

HOW TO MAKE TACO FILLING

Ingredients

- 1 lb lean ground beef
- 1 onion, diced
- 1/2 cup ketchup
- 1 package taco seasoning mix
- 2/3 cup cold water

Directions

- Cook ground beef and onion over medium heat before stirring in ketchup, cold water and taco seasoning, and cooking all this for 20 minutes at low heat.
- Serve.

Serving: 4

Timing Information:

Preparation	Cooking	Total Time
5 mins	25 mins	30 mins

Nutritional Information:

Calories	371 kcal
Carbohydrates	16.4 g
Cholesterol	85 mg
Fat	23.6 g
Fiber	0.5 g
Protein	21 g
Sodium	1060 mg

* Percent Daily Values are based on a 2,000 calorie diet.

Meatball Sub

Ingredients

- 1 1/2 lbs lean ground beef
- 1/3 C. Italian seasoned bread crumbs
- 1/2 small onion, diced
- 1 tsp salt
- 1/2 C. shredded mozzarella cheese, divided
- 1 tbsp cracked black pepper
- 1 tsp garlic powder
- 1/2 C. marinara sauce
- 3 hoagie rolls, split lengthwise

Directions

- Set your oven to 350 degrees before doing anything else.
- Get a bowl, combine: 1/2 of the mozzarella, beef, garlic powder, bread crumbs, pepper, onions, and salt.
- Shape the mix into a large loaf then place it in a casserole dish.
- Cook the meat in the oven for 55 mins then let it cool for 10 mins.

- Cut the meat into slices then layer the pieces of meat on a roll.
- Top everything with the marinara then add a topping of cheese.
- Cover the sandwich with some foil and put everything in the oven for 20 more mins.
- Let the sandwich cool for 20 mins then cut each one in half.
- Enjoy.

Amount per serving (6 total)

Timing Information:

Preparation	15 m
Cooking	1 h 5 m
Total Time	1 h 40 m

Nutritional Information:

Calories	491 kcal
Fat	21.4 g
Carbohydrates	43.1g
Protein	29.3 g
Cholesterol	75 mg
Sodium	1068 mg

* Percent Daily Values are based on a 2,000 calorie diet.

Chicken and Onions

Ingredients

- 1 lb skinless, boneless chicken breast halves - cut into strips
- 1 tbsp vegetable oil
- 1 onion, sliced into strips
- 2 tbsps salsa
- 10 (10 inch) flour tortillas
- 2 C. shredded Cheddar-Monterey Jack cheese blend

Directions

- Coat a baking sheet with nonstick spray. Then set your oven to 350 degrees before anything else.
- Stir fry your chicken until fully done. Then combine in your onions and cook until they are see-through. Then add your salsa and shut off the heat.
- For 1 min in the microwave warm your tortillas.
- On one side of each tortilla layer it with cheese and chicken.
- Fold over the other side to form a quesadilla.

- Do this for all ingredients and tortillas.
- Place everything on the greased sheet and cook in the oven for until the cheese is bubbly.
- Enjoy.

Amount per serving (10 total)

Timing Information:

Preparation	Cooking	Total Time
20 m	7 m	27 m

Nutritional Information:

Calories	381 kcal
Fat	8.4 g
Carbohydrates	42.1g
Protein	21.7 g
Cholesterol	46 mg
Sodium	530 mg

* Percent Daily Values are based on a 2,000 calorie diet.

Authentic Tomato Sauce

Use this sauce a topping for any type of pasta. Remember, to make pasta get your water boiling in a big pot. Then once it is boiling, add your pasta to the water and let it boil for 9 minutes.

Ingredients

- 2 tbsp olive oil
- 6 garlic cloves (minced)
- 2 tsp chili flakes, optional
- 1 (28 oz.) cans crushed tomatoes
- 1/2 C. water
- 1/4 C. fresh basil (chopped)
- 1 tsp salt

Directions

- In a frying pan, cook the oil, chili flakes and garlic on medium-high heat till just aromatic.
- Stir in the tomatoes, 1/2 of the basil and salt and bring to a boil.
- Add the water and reduce the heat, then simmer for about 1 hour.

- Serve with a garnishing of the remaining basil alongside the pasta of your choice.

Amount per serving: 4

Timing Information:

Preparation	10 mins
Total Time	1 hr 40 mins

Nutritional Information:

Calories	122.1
Fat	7.3g
Cholesterol	0.0mg
Sodium	1021.4mg
Carbohydrates	14.6g
Protein	2.0g

* Percent Daily Values are based on a 2,000 calorie diet.

A Hearty Homemade Tomato Spaghetti

Ingredients

- 12 oz. spaghetti
- 1 lb. lean ground beef
- 1 tsp salt
- 3/4 tsp white sugar
- 1 tsp dried oregano
- 1/4 tsp ground black pepper
- 1/8 tsp garlic powder
- 2 tbsp dried minced onion, optional
- 2 1/2 C. chopped tomatoes
- 1 1/3 (6 oz.) cans tomato paste
- 1 (4.5 oz.) can sliced mushrooms, optional

Directions

- Heat a skillet and cook the beef on medium heat till browned completely and drain off the excess fat.
- In a large pan, add the beef and the remaining ingredients except pasta and simmer, stirring occasionally for about 2 hours.
- Cook the spaghetti according to the package's directions and drain well.
- Pour the sauce over the spaghetti and serve.

Amount per serving (5 total)

Timing Information:

Preparation	15m
Cooking	2 h
Total Time	2h 15m

Nutritional Information:

Calories	557 kcal
Fat	20.3 g
Carbohydrates	65.7g
Protein	28.2 g
Cholesterol	68 mg
Sodium	1002 mg

* Percent Daily Values are based on a 2,000 calorie diet.

Mediterranean Salad

Ingredients

- 3 cucumbers, seeded and sliced
- 1 1/2 C. crumbled feta cheese
- 1 C. black olives, pitted and sliced
- 3 C. diced roma tomatoes
- 1/3 C. diced oil packed sun-dried tomatoes, drained, oil reserved
- 1/2 red onion, sliced

Directions

- Get a bowl, combine: 2 tbsps sun dried tomato oil, red onions, cucumbers, sundried tomatoes, feta, roma tomatoes, and olives.
- Place a covering of plastic around the bowl and put everything in the fridge until it is cold.
- Enjoy.

Amount per serving (8 total)

Timing Information:

Preparation	
Cooking	10 m
Total Time	10 m

Nutritional Information:

Calories	131 kcal
Fat	8.8 g
Carbohydrates	9.3g
Protein	5.5 g
Cholesterol	25 mg
Sodium	486 mg

* Percent Daily Values are based on a 2,000 calorie diet.

Classical Potato Salad

Ingredients

- 2 lbs clean, scrubbed new red potatoes
- 6 eggs
- 1 lb bacon
- 1 onion, finely diced
- 1 stalk celery, finely diced
- 2 C. mayonnaise
- salt and pepper to taste

Directions

- Boil your potatoes in water and salt for 20 mins then remove the liquids.
- Once the potatoes are no longer hot, chop them, with the skins.
- Now get your eggs boiling in water for 60 secs, place a lid on the pot, and shut the heat.
- Let the eggs sit for 15 mins. Then remove the shells and dice them.
- Stir fry your bacon until it is crispy then break it into pieces.

- Get a bowl, combine: black pepper, celery, salt, eggs, mayo, onion, and bacon.
- Place a covering of plastic around the bowl and put everything in the fridge for 65 mins.
- Enjoy.

Amount per serving (12 total)

Timing Information:

Preparation	
Cooking	1 h
Total Time	2 h

Nutritional Information:

Calories	430 kcal
Fat	36.9 g
Carbohydrates	16.2g
Protein	9.5 g
Cholesterol	121 mg
Sodium	536 mg

* Percent Daily Values are based on a 2,000 calorie diet.

Easy Spinach Salad

Ingredients

- 2 bunches spinach, rinsed and torn into bite-size pieces
- 4 C. sliced strawberries
- 1/2 C. vegetable oil
- 1/4 C. white wine vinegar
- 1/2 C. white sugar
- 1/4 tsp paprika
- 2 tbsps sesame seeds
- 1 tbsp poppy seeds

Directions

- Get a bowl, combine: strawberries and spinach.
- Get a 2nd bowl, combine: poppy seeds, oil, sesame seeds, vinegar, paprika, and sugar.
- Combine both bowls then serve the salad.
- Enjoy.

Amount per serving (8 total)

Timing Information:

Preparation	
Cooking	10 m
Total Time	10 m

Nutritional Information:

Calories	235 kcal
Fat	15.9 g
Carbohydrates	22.8g
Protein	3.6 g
Cholesterol	0 mg
Sodium	69 mg

* Percent Daily Values are based on a 2,000 calorie diet.

EGG SALAD

Ingredients

- 8 eggs
- 1/2 C. mayonnaise
- 1 tsp prepared yellow mustard
- 1/4 C. diced green onion
- salt and pepper to taste
- 1/4 tsp paprika

Directions

- Boil your eggs in water for 2 mins then place a lid on the pot and let the contents sit for 15 mins. Once the eggs have cooled remove their shells and dice them.
- Now get a bowl, combine: green onions, eggs, mustard, and mayo.
- Stir the mix until it is smooth then add in the paprika, pepper, and salt.
- Stir the contents again then enjoy with toasted buns.

Amount per serving (4 total)

Timing Information:

Preparation	10 m
Cooking	15 m
Total Time	35 m

Nutritional Information:

Calories	344 kcal
Fat	31.9 g
Carbohydrates	2.3g
Protein	< 13 g
Cholesterol	382 mg
Sodium	1351 mg

* Percent Daily Values are based on a 2,000 calorie diet.

Simply Baked Pear Dessert

Ingredients

- 4 Bosc pears
- 2 tbsps honey
- 3 tbsps butter, melted
- dash ground ginger

Directions

- Preheat your oven at 375 degrees F and put some oil over the quiche dish.
- Peel and cut a portion off of the bottom of your pears so that they can stand straight, and place them in the baking dish.
- Pour melted butter, honey and some ground ginger over these pears before covering the dish with aluminum foil.
- Bake in the preheated oven for about one hour or until the top is golden brown in color.

Serving: 4

Timing Information:

Preparation	Cooking	Total Time
15 mins	1 hr	1 hr 30 mins

Nutritional Information:

Calories	206 kcal
Carbohydrates	34.5 g
Cholesterol	23 mg
Fat	8.9 g
Fiber	5.2 g
Protein	0.8 g
Sodium	64 mg

* Percent Daily Values are based on a 2,000 calorie diet.

THE SIMPLEST ZUCCHINI QUICHE I

Ingredients

- 2 cups grated zucchini
- 1 (9 inch) pie shell, unbaked
- 6 eggs, beaten
- 1 cup shredded Cheddar cheese

Directions

- Preheat your oven at 350 degrees F and put some oil over the quiche dish.
- Put zucchini evenly in quiche dish before adding eggs and some cheddar cheese.
- Bake in the preheated oven for about 30 minutes or until the top of the quiche is golden brown in color.

Serving: 9

Timing Information:

Preparation	Cooking	Total Time
15 mins	30 mins	45 mins

Nutritional Information:

Calories	314 kcal
Carbohydrates	15.7 g
Cholesterol	188 mg
Fat	22 g
Fiber	1.6 g
Protein	13.6 g
Sodium	364 mg

* Percent Daily Values are based on a 2,000 calorie diet.

A Classic Quiche

Ingredients

- 1 tbsp butter
- 1 large onion, diced
- 3 eggs
- 1/3 cup heavy cream
- 1/3 cup shredded Swiss cheese
- 1 (9 inch pie) unbaked pie crust

Directions

- Preheat your oven to 375 degrees F and put some oil over the quiche dish.
- Melt butter over medium heat and then cook onions in it until soft.
- Now whisk eggs and cream together in a bowl and then add cheese.
- Place onion at the bottom of the dish and pour this mixture over it.
- Bake in the preheated oven for about 30 minutes or until the top of the quiche is golden brown in color.

Serving: 8

Timing Information:

Preparation	Cooking	Total Time
10 mins	30 mins	40 mins

Nutritional Information:

Calories	212 kcal
Carbohydrates	12.7 g
Cholesterol	91 mg
Fat	15.7 g
Fiber	1.1 g
Protein	5.4 g
Sodium	211 mg

* Percent Daily Values are based on a 2,000 calorie diet.

CHICKEN & DUMPLINGS

Ingredients:

- 2 (10.5 ounce) cans cream of chicken soup
- 3 (14 ounce) cans chicken broth
- 3 cups shredded cooked chicken meat
- 2 (10 ounce) cans refrigerated biscuit dough

Directions:

- Heat a mixture of chicken soup, shredded chicken and chicken broth in saucepan until it is simmering.
- Slice biscuits in four parts and place them in this hot soup.
- Turn the heat down to low and cook for another 15 minutes.
- Serve.

Serving: 8

Timing Information:

Preparation	Cooking	Total Time
5 mins	15 mins	20 mins

Nutritional Information:

Calories	400 kcal
Carbohydrates	36.4 g
Cholesterol	50 mg
Fat	18.1 g
Fiber	0.5 g
Protein	21.5 g
Sodium	1924 mg

* Percent Daily Values are based on a 2,000 calorie diet.

POTATO DUMPLINGS

Ingredients:

- 4 large potatoes
- 1 cup all-purpose flour
- 1 tsp salt

Directions:

- Grate peeled potatoes with the help of a food processor and then add some salt and flour into it to form a dough.
- Now place dumplings made with the help of a spoon into some boiling water.
- Make sure that the dumplings aren't sticking together in the first few minutes.
- Now turn the heat down to low and cook these dumplings for the next 40 minutes.
- Take them out and serve with melted butter or gravy of some kind.

Serving: 4

Timing Information:

Preparation	Cooking	Total Time
15 mins	40 mins	55 mins

Nutritional Information:

Calories	398 kcal
Carbohydrates	88.3 g
Cholesterol	0 mg
Fat	0.6 g
Fiber	9 g
Protein	10.7 g
Sodium	604 mg

* Percent Daily Values are based on a 2,000 calorie diet.

Classical Empanada I

Ingredients

- 1/2 cup butter, softened
- 1 (3 ounce) package cream cheese
- 1 cup sifted all-purpose flour
- 1 cup fruit preserves
- 1/3 cup white sugar

Directions

- Whisk butter, flour and cream together until smooth before shaping it up and wrapping it in foil to be placed in the refrigerator for at least one night.
- Set your oven to 375 degrees F.
- Roll the dough on a floured surface before cutting it with a cookie cutter and placing jam in the center of each one.
- Bake this in the preheated oven for about 20 minutes before coating it with the mixture of sugar.

Serving: 12

Timing Information:

Preparation	Cooking	Total Time
15 mins	25 mins	40 mins

Nutritional Information:

Calories	226 kcal
Carbohydrates	32.1 g
Cholesterol	28 mg
Fat	10.3 g
Fiber	0.7 g
Protein	1.8 g
Sodium	84 mg

* Percent Daily Values are based on a 2,000 calorie diet.

The Quickest Mac 'n' Cheese

Ingredients

- 1 cup macaroni
- 1/2 cup process cheese sauce
- 2 frankfurters, sliced
- 1 tsp grated Parmesan cheese
- 4 buttery round crackers, crushed

Directions

- Set your oven at 350 degrees F.
- Cook pasta in salty boiling water for about 10 minutes until tender before draining it.
- Heat up cheese sauce in microwave for about 1 minute before baking the mixture of cooked pasta, cheese sauce, parmesan and sliced frankfurters for about 10 minutes.
- Serve.

Serving: 4

Timing Information:

Preparation	Cooking	Total Time
2 mins	13 mins	15 mins

Nutritional Information:

Calories	284 kcal
Carbohydrates	25.9 g
Cholesterol	36 mg
Fat	14.9 g
Fiber	1.5 g
Protein	10.8 g
Sodium	829 mg

* Percent Daily Values are based on a 2,000 calorie diet.

American Mac and Cheese

Ingredients

- 2 pounds uncooked elbow macaroni
- 2 (10.75 ounce) cans condensed Cheddar cheese soup
- 4 eggs, beaten
- 2 3/4 cups milk
- 2 pounds Cheddar cheese, shredded, divided

Directions

- Set your oven at 400 degrees F and also put some oil on the baking dish.
- Cook macaroni in boiling water for about 8 minutes before draining it with the help of a colander.
- Pour the mixture of cooked macaroni, cheese, milk, eggs, pepper and soup into the baking dish.
- Top all this with the remaining cheese.
- Bake this in the preheated oven for about 45 minutes covered and 15 minutes uncovered or until the top begins to turn brown.

Serving: 16

Timing Information:

Preparation	Cooking	Total Time
10 mins	1 hr 10 mins	1 hr 20 mins

Nutritional Information:

Calories	537 kcal
Carbohydrates	49.6 g
Cholesterol	118 mg
Fat	25.3 g
Fiber	2.9 g
Protein	26.9 g
Sodium	669 mg

* Percent Daily Values are based on a 2,000 calorie diet.

MAC AND CHEESE PIZZA

Ingredients

- 1 (12 inch) pre-baked pizza crust
- 3/4 cup cavatappi (corkscrew macaroni)
- 2/3 (16 ounce) jar cheese sauce (such as Ragu® Double Cheddar), divided, or as needed
- 1 tbsps butter
- 1/2 cup shredded Cheddar cheese

Directions

- Set your oven at 450 degrees F and put pizza crust on a baking dish.
- Cook cavatappi in boiling salty water for about 11 minutes before draining and putting it back in the pot.
- Add cheese sauce and butter into the pot, and cook until you see that butter has melted and everything is thoroughly combined.
- Add cheese sauce, shredded cheddar cheese, pasta- cheese mixture and remaining cheese sauce respectively over the pizza crust in the baking dish.

- Bake this in the preheated oven for about 10 minutes.
- Let it stand as it is for about 2 minutes before slicing it into pieces.

Serving: 4

Timing Information:

Preparation	Cooking	Total Time
10 mins	25 mins	35 mins

Nutritional Information:

Calories	584 kcal
Carbohydrates	64.6 g
Cholesterol	59 mg
Fat	26 g
Fiber	2.5 g
Protein	25.9 g
Sodium	1186 mg

* Percent Daily Values are based on a 2,000 calorie diet.

Monterey Shrimp

Ingredients

- 1 (8 ounce) package Monterey Jack cheese, cut into strips
- 40 large shrimp - peeled, deveined and butterflied
- 20 slices bacon, cut in half

Directions

- Set your oven at 450 degrees F.
- Put cheese along with a slice of bacon in the butter flied opening of each shrimp before placing it on a cookie sheet.
- Bake this in the preheated oven for about 15 minutes.
- Serve.

Serving: 8

Timing Information:

Preparation	Cooking	Total Time
20 mins	10 mins	30 mins

Nutritional Information:

Calories	284 kcal
Carbohydrates	0.4 g
Cholesterol	205 mg
Fat	16.9 g
Fiber	0 g
Protein	30.7 g
Sodium	753 mg

* Percent Daily Values are based on a 2,000 calorie diet.

Italian Cabbage II

Ingredients

- 1 large head cabbage, finely chopped
- 1 (14.5 ounce) can diced tomatoes with juice
- 1 onion, halved and thinly sliced
- 1 tbsp Italian seasoning
- 1 lb lean ground beef

Directions

- Cook a mixture of cabbage, Italian seasoning, tomatoes with juice, and onion over low heat for a few minutes before adding ground beef and cooking all this for 45 minutes or until the cabbage is tender.
- Serve.

Timing Information:

Preparation	Cooking	Total Time
10 mins	35 mins	45 mins

Nutritional Information:

Calories	228 kcal
Carbohydrates	18.3 g
Cholesterol	50 mg
Fat	9.5 g
Fiber	6.7 g
Protein	18.1 g
Sodium	255 mg

* Percent Daily Values are based on a 2,000 calorie diet.

Ground Beef Macaroni

Ingredients

- 1 1/2 lbs lean ground beef
- 1 green bell pepper, diced
- 1 onion, diced
- 2 (29 ounce) cans tomato sauce
- 1 (16 ounce) package macaroni

Directions

- Cook pasta according to the directions of package before draining it using a colander.
- Cook ground beef over medium heat until brown before adding chopped onion and cooking it for another few minutes to get them soft.
- Now add tomato sauce and green pepper before cooking it until pepper is soft.
- Pour this sauce over pasta for serving.

Serving: 6

Timing Information:

Preparation	Cooking	Total Time
30 mins	30 mins	1 hr

Nutritional Information:

Calories	570 kcal
Carbohydrates	72.9 g
Cholesterol	74 mg
Fat	15.5 g
Fiber	6.8 g
Protein	35.2 g
Sodium	1492 mg

* Percent Daily Values are based on a 2,000 calorie diet.

BUTTERED SALMON

Ingredients

- 1 pound salmon fillets or steaks
- 1/2 tsp ground black pepper
- 1 tsp onion powder
- 1 tsp dried dill weed
- 2 tbsps butter

Directions

- Set your oven at 400 degrees before doing anything else.
- Coat salmon with onion powder, pepper, butter and dill very thoroughly before placing it in the oven.
- Bake this in the preheated oven for about 25 minutes.
- Serve.

Serving: 4

Timing Information:

Preparation	Cooking	Total Time
5 mins	25 mins	30 mins

Nutritional Information:

Calories	262 kcal
Carbohydrates	0.7 g
Cholesterol	82 mg
Fat	18.1 g
Fiber	0.1 g
Protein	22.8 g
Sodium	254 mg

* Percent Daily Values are based on a 2,000 calorie diet.

GINGER AND GRAPEFRUIT SALMON

Ingredients

- 1/2 grapefruit, juiced
- 3 1/3 ounces soy sauce
- 1/2 tsp garlic powder
- 1/4 tsp ground ginger
- 1 whole salmon fillet

Directions

- Set your oven at 400 degrees before doing anything else.
- Coat salmon with a mixture of grapefruit juice, ground ginger, soy sauce, and garlic powder before covering it with plastic wrap and refrigerating it for at least one hour.
- Bake this in the preheated oven for about 40 minutes.
- Serve.

Serving: 1

Timing Information:

Preparation	Cooking	Total Time
10 mins	40 mins	1 hr 50 mins

Nutritional Information:

Calories	221 kcal
Carbohydrates	2.9 g
Cholesterol	66 mg
Fat	12.2 g
Fiber	0.2 g
Protein	23.4 g
Sodium	1040 mg

* Percent Daily Values are based on a 2,000 calorie diet.

CHICKEN CUTLETS

Ingredients

- 4 skinless, boneless chicken breast halves - pounded to 1/2 inch thickness
- 2 tbsps all-purpose flour
- 1 egg, beaten
- 1 cup panko bread crumbs
- 1 cup oil for frying, or as needed

Directions

- Get three bowls. Bowl 1 for chicken. Bowl 2 for bread crumbs. Bowl 3 for eggs.
- Cover chicken with flour first. Then with egg, and finally with crumbs.
- Get a frying pan and heat 1/4 inch of oil. Fry your chicken for 5 mins on each side.
- Remove excess oil.
- Enjoy.

Servings: 4 servings

Timing Information:

Preparation	Cooking	Total Time
10 mins	10 mins	20 mins

Nutritional Information:

Calories	297 kcal
Carbohydrates	22.2 g
Cholesterol	118 mg
Fat	11.4 g
Fiber	0.1 g
Protein	31.2 g
Sodium	251 mg

* Percent Daily Values are based on a 2,000 calorie diet.

CROCK POT OATMEAL I

Ingredients

- 1 C. steel cut oats
- 3 1/2 C. water
- 1 C. peeled and chopped apple
- 1/2 C. raisins
- 2 tbsps butter
- 1 tbsp ground cinnamon
- 2 tbsps brown sugar
- 1 tsp vanilla extract

Directions

- For 7 hours on low cook the following in your crock pot: vanilla extract, oats, brown sugar, water, cinnamon, apples, butter, and raisins.
- Enjoy with milk.

Amount per serving (6 total)

Timing Information:

Preparation	Cooking	Total Time
15 m	6 h	6 h 15 m

Nutritional Information:

Calories	208 kcal
Fat	5.6 g
Carbohydrates	37.2g
Protein	3.9 g
Cholesterol	10 mg
Sodium	35 mg

* Percent Daily Values are based on a 2,000 calorie diet.

CRANBERRY MAPLE OATMEAL

Ingredients

- 3 1/2 C. plain or vanilla soy milk
- 1/4 tsp salt
- 2 C. rolled oats
- 1/4 C. pure maple syrup
- 1/3 C. raisins
- 1/3 C. dried cranberries
- 1/3 C. sweetened flaked coconut
- 1/3 C. chopped walnuts
- 1 (8 oz.) container plain yogurt (optional)
- 3 tbsps honey (optional)

Directions

- Boil your milk in a large pan. Then combine in cranberries, oats, raisins, and maple syrup.
- Let this cook, boiling, for 6 mins. Then shut off the heat and add in your coconuts and walnuts.

- Before eating add a dollop of honey and yogurt.
- Enjoy.

Amount per serving (6 total)

Timing Information:

Preparation	Cooking	Total Time
5 m	10 m	15 m

Nutritional Information:

Calories	379 kcal
Fat	10.4 g
Carbohydrates	63.1g
Protein	11.6 g
Cholesterol	2 mg
Sodium	212 mg

* Percent Daily Values are based on a 2,000 calorie diet.

Waffle II

(Vanilla)

Ingredients

- 2 eggs
- 2 C. all-purpose flour
- 1 3/4 C. milk
- 1/2 C. vegetable oil
- 1 tbsp white sugar
- 4 tsps baking powder
- 1/4 tsp salt
- 1/2 tsp vanilla extract

Directions

- Get your waffle iron hot.
- Get a bowl, mix evenly: whisk eggs, veggie oil, vanilla, flour, salt, milk, baking powder, and sugar.

- Coat your iron with nonstick spray. Ladle batter onto the iron. Cook until golden enjoy.

Servings: 6 servings

Timing Information:

Preparation	Cooking	Total Time
5 mins	15 mins	20 mins

Nutritional Information:

Calories	382 kcal
Carbohydrates	38 g
Cholesterol	68 mg
Fat	21.6 g
Fiber	1.1 g
Protein	8.7 g
Sodium	390 mg

* Percent Daily Values are based on a 2,000 calorie diet.

Easy Buttermilk Waffle

Ingredients

- 2 1/4 C. flour
- 1 tsp baking soda
- 1 tsp baking powder
- 1/2 tsp salt
- 1/4 C. butter
- 1/4 C. brown sugar
- 3 egg yolks
- 2 C. buttermilk
- 3 egg whites

Directions

- Get your waffle iron hot.
- Get a bowl, mix evenly: salt, flour, baking powder and soda.
- Get a 2nd bowl, mix: brown sugar, whisked eggs, cream butter, buttermilk.
- Combine bowl 1 and 2 to form a batter.

- Get a 3rd bowl: Beat egg whites until stiff (an upward motion from the whisk produces a peak).
- Mix in 1/3 of your eggs into the batter until smooth. Then add the rest. Continue mixing until completely smooth.
- Coat your iron with nonstick spray. Ladle batter onto the iron. Cook until crispy.
- Enjoy warm.

Servings: 6 waffles

Timing Information:

Preparation	Cooking	Total Time
15 mins	5 mins	45 mins

Nutritional Information:

Calories	329 kcal
Carbohydrates	46.2 g
Cholesterol	126 mg
Fat	11.1 g
Fiber	1.3 g
Protein	10.8 g
Sodium	638 mg

* Percent Daily Values are based on a 2,000 calorie diet.

WAFFLE III
(POTATOES)

Ingredients

- 2 tbsps butter
- 1 onion, chopped
- 1 tbsp minced garlic
- 2 C. mashed potatoes
- 1/4 C. all-purpose flour
- 2 eggs
- 1/4 tsp salt
- 1/4 tsp ground black pepper

Directions

- Get a frying pan. Heat it up. Then melt your butter. Stir fry garlic and onions for 8 mins.
- Get your waffle iron hot.

- Get a bowl, evenly mix: black pepper, fried garlic and onions, salt, mashed potatoes, eggs, flour, and salt.
- Coat your iron with nonstick spray.
- With a batch process cook 1/3 C. of batter on the iron until crispy (4 mins usually).
- Continue for all batter.
- Enjoy warm.

Servings: 4 servings

Timing Information:

Preparation	Cooking	Total Time
10 mins	15 mins	25 mins

Nutritional Information:

Calories	217 kcal
Carbohydrates	27.9 g
Cholesterol	110 mg
Fat	9 g
Fiber	2.3 g
Protein	6.5 g
Sodium	540 mg

* Percent Daily Values are based on a 2,000 calorie diet.

THE SIMPLE FRITTATA FORMULA

Ingredients

- 2 large eggs
- salt
- fresh ground pepper
- 2 tbsps shredded cheese
- 2/3 C. vegetables
- 2 tbsps fresh herbs

Directions

- Set your oven to 350 degrees before doing anything else.
- Get a bowl, combine: herbs, cheese, and eggs.
- Coat a skillet with nonstick spray then add in your veggies.
- Cook the veggies for 1 min then add in the egg mix.
- Set the heat to low and let the bottom of the eggs set with a lid on the pan for 10 mins.
- Now place the frittata in the oven for 5 to 10 more mins until the top is set.

- Enjoy.

Servings Per Recipe: 1

Timing Information:

Preparation	5 mins
Total Time	25 mins

Nutritional Information:

Calories	239.0 kcal
Cholesterol	440.7mg
Sodium	408.4mg
Carbohydrates	3.0g
Protein	18.0g

* Percent Daily Values are based on a 2,000 calorie diet.

Golden State Frittata

Ingredients

- 3 tsps olive oil, divided
- 2 C. sliced onions or 2 C. scallions or 2 C. leeks, or combination
- coarse salt
- fresh ground pepper
- 1 C. tomatoes
- 6 egg whites
- 4 egg yolks, beaten
- 4 oz. cheese

Directions

- Set your oven to 350 degrees before doing anything else.
- Begin to stir fry your scallions after topping them with pepper and salt for 60 secs then place a lid on the pot and cook the mix for 6 mins.
- Combine in the tomatoes and place the lid back on the pot for 3 more mins.

- Now place everything into a bowl.
- Get a 2nd bowl and whisk some pepper, some salt, and the egg whites until the mix is peaking.
- Now combine in the yolks slowly.
- Coat your frying pan with 1 tsp of olive oil then pour in the eggs into the pan evenly, making sure that the entire surface is covered.
- Now top the eggs with the tomato mix and leave about 1 inch of space on the edge of the frittata.
- Top everything with the cheese and fry the mix for about 4 mins then place it in the oven for 22 mins until it is fully done.
- Enjoy.

Servings Per Recipe: 4

Timing Information:

| Preparation | 15 mins |
| Total Time | 50 mins |

Nutritional Information:

Calories	238.9 kcal
Cholesterol	369.3mg
Sodium	12.5g
Carbohydrates	14.6g
Protein	238.9 kcal

* Percent Daily Values are based on a 2,000 calorie diet.

THE NEW YORKER FRITTATA

Ingredients

- 4 slices bacon, crumbled
- 1 1/2 C. potatoes, cubed
- 1 onion, chopped
- 6 eggs
- 1/2 C. water
- 1/2 tsp salt
- 1/4 tsp black pepper
- 2 C. frozen broccoli, thawed
- 3/4 C. cheddar cheese, shredded

Directions

- Fry your bacon for 7 mins then combine in the onions and potatoes. Place a lid on the pan and let everything cook for 8 mins. Stir the mix at least twice as it cooks.
- Now get a bowl and combine: 1/2 C. cheese, eggs, broccoli, 1/2 C. water, 1/4 tsp pepper, 1/2 tsp salt.

- Whisk the mix until it is smooth then pour it into the pan. Place the lid back on the pan and cook everything with a medium level of heat for 9 mins.
- Shut the heat and top the mix with the cheese and place the lid back on the pan.
- Once the cheese has melted serve.
- Enjoy.

Servings Per Recipe: 4

Timing Information:

Preparation	5 mins
Total Time	25 mins

Nutritional Information:

Calories	304.2 kcal
Cholesterol	306.6mg
Sodium	619.5mg
Carbohydrates	17.0g
Protein	19.2g

* Percent Daily Values are based on a 2,000 calorie diet.

THE SIMPLE CHIVES FRITTATA

Ingredients

- 8 eggs
- 2 tbsps water
- 1 C. shredded colby-monterey jack cheese, divided
- 1/2 C. fresh chives, chopped
- 1/2 C. minced red bell pepper
- 1/2 tsp fresh ground black pepper

Directions

- Set your oven to 350 degrees before doing anything else.
- Get a bowl and beat your eggs in it then add in: 1/2 C. of cheese, herbs, black pepper, and bell pepper.
- Combine the mix until it is smooth then coat a pie dish with nonstick spray.
- Add the wet mix to the pan and evenly then top it with the rest of the cheese.

- Cook the frittata in the oven for 35 mins then top it with some more herbs.
- Enjoy.

Servings Per Recipe: 8

Timing Information:

Preparation	10 mins
Total Time	40 mins

Nutritional Information:

Calories	128.9 kcal
Cholesterol	224.0mg
Sodium	146.0mg
Carbohydrates	1.1g
Protein	9.8g

* Percent Daily Values are based on a 2,000 calorie diet.

Simply Baked Broccoli

Ingredients

- 1 (12 oz.) bag broccoli florets
- 1/2 red onion, sliced
- 8 fresh sage leaves, torn
- 2 tbsps extra-virgin olive oil
- 1/2 tsp salt
- 1/2 tsp garlic salt
- 1/4 tsp ground black pepper

Directions

- Cover a casserole dish or sheet for baking with foil and then set your oven to 400 degrees before doing anything else.
- Layer your broccoli evenly throughout the dish and top with sage leaves and onions. Garnish all the veggies with olive oil and then black pepper, regular salt, and garlic salt.
- Cook the veggies in the oven for 27 mins until slightly browned and crunchy.

- Enjoy.

Amount per serving (4 total)

Timing Information:

Preparation	Cooking	Total Time
10 m	20 m	30 m

Nutritional Information:

Calories	97 kcal
Fat	7.1 g
Carbohydrates	7.3g
Protein	2.6 g
Cholesterol	0 mg
Sodium	546 mg

* Percent Daily Values are based on a 2,000 calorie diet.

CRACKERS AND BROCCOLI BAKE

Ingredients

- 2 (10 oz.) packages frozen chopped broccoli
- 8 oz. processed cheese food, shredded
- 1/4 lb butter
- 32 buttery round crackers, crushed

Directions

- Set your oven to 350 degrees before doing anything else.
- Layer your broccoli in a baking dish then top the veggies with the processed cheese.
- Now begin to stir fry your crushed crackers in butter, for 1 min, while stirring, then top the broccoli with the mix.
- Cook everything in the oven for 35 mins.
- Enjoy.

Amount per serving (8 total)

Timing Information:

Preparation	Cooking	Total Time
10 m	40 m	50 m

Nutritional Information:

Calories	330 kcal
Fat	25.6 g
Carbohydrates	16g
Protein	9.4 g
Cholesterol	56 mg
Sodium	577 mg

* Percent Daily Values are based on a 2,000 calorie diet.

Yellow Fritters

Ingredients

- 1 1/3 C. buttermilk baking mix
- 1 1/2 tsps baking powder
- 1 (14.75 oz.) can cream-style corn
- 1 egg, beaten
- 1 C. vegetable oil
- 1 1/2 C. molasses

Directions

- Get a bowl, combine: baking powder and baking mix.
- Get a 2nd bowl, combine: eggs and corn.
- Now combine both bowls and get your oil hot and ready for frying.
- Once the oil is hot fry large dollops of the mix for 3 mins each side or until golden on both sides.
- When eating the fritters top them with some molasses.
- Enjoy.

Amount per serving (16 total)

Timing Information:

Preparation	10 m
Cooking	30 m
Total Time	50 m

Nutritional Information:

Calories	255 kcal
Fat	14.4 g
Carbohydrates	31.9g
Protein	1.7 g
Cholesterol	12 mg
Sodium	319 mg

* Percent Daily Values are based on a 2,000 calorie diet.

Simple Cream of Meatball

Ingredients

- 5 pounds Italian meatballs
- 1 (10.75 oz.) can condensed cream of mushroom soup
- 3/4 C. water
- 2 C. sour cream

Directions

- Get a container and mix your sour cream, meatballs, water, and mushroom together. Place a lid on the container and place it in the fridge for 8 hrs.
- Now add everything to your slow cooker and cook for about 3 to 4 hours on medium until the meat is completely cooked.

Servings: 20 servings

Timing Information:

Preparation	Cooking	Total Time
8 hrs 5 mins	1 hr	9 hrs 5 mins

Nutritional Information:

Calories	427 kcal
Carbohydrates	8.8 g
Cholesterol	98 mg
Fat	35.4 g
Fiber	2.7 g
Protein	17.2 g
Sodium	962 mg

* Percent Daily Values are based on a 2,000 calorie diet.

Vegetarian Meatballs II

Ingredients

- 1 (8 oz.) package tempeh, cut into 4 pieces
- 2 slices whole grain bread
- 3 tbsps grated Parmesan cheese
- 1 egg, lightly beaten
- 1 tbsp dried parsley
- 1 tsp dried oregano
- 1 tsp dried basil
- 1/2 tsp garlic powder
- 1/4 tsp salt
- 1/4 tsp freshly ground black pepper
- 1 pinch red pepper flakes, your preferred amount

Directions

- Set your oven to 350 degrees before doing anything else.
- Boil your tempeh in water for 7 mins. Remove excess water and set aside.

- Pulse your bread in a food processor, then mix the following in a bowl: red pepper flakes, crumbled tempeh, black pepper, parmesan, salt, pulsed bread, garlic powder, whisked eggs, basil, oregano, and parsley.
- Make your tempeh into golf sized balls.
- Set in a dish and cook for 12 mins in the oven. Turn the tempeh pieces and bake for 10 additional mins.

Servings: 20 meatballs

Timing Information:

Preparation	Cooking	Total Time
15 mins	25 mins	40 mins

Nutritional Information:

Calories	73 kcal
Carbohydrates	4.9 g
Cholesterol	20 mg
Fat	3.6 g
Fiber	0.6 g
Protein	6.2 g
Sodium	113 mg

* Percent Daily Values are based on a 2,000 calorie diet.

MAKE A MEATBALL SOUP

Ingredients

- 2 quarts water
- 20 pre-packaged meatballs
- 2 (8 oz.) cans tomato sauce
- 2 cubes beef bouillon cube
- 1/2 tsp dried oregano
- 1/2 tsp dried basil
- 1/4 tsp dried thyme
- salt to taste
- ground black pepper to taste
- 2 stalks celery, sliced
- 2 carrots, sliced
- 1 clove garlic, diced
- 1 C. elbow macaroni

Directions

- Boil, then simmer the following for 35 mins: garlic, meatballs, pepper, tomato sauce, salt, bouillon, celery, oregano, carrots, thyme, and basil.
- After simmering time has elapsed combine in your macaroni, and let it cook until al dente.
- Garnish the soup with parmesan.
- Enjoy after cooling a bit.

Servings: 6 -8 servings

Timing Information:

Preparation	Cooking	Total Time
10 mins	50 mins	1 hr

Nutritional Information:

Calories	255 kcal
Carbohydrates	22.5 g
Cholesterol	66 mg
Fat	10.7 g
Fiber	2.6 g
Protein	16.7 g
Sodium	713 mg

* Percent Daily Values are based on a 2,000 calorie diet.

GROUND BEEF FESTIVAL

Ingredients

- 1 lb ground beef
- 1 tbsp garlic pepper seasoning
- 1 (15 ounce) can corn, drained
- 1 cup ranch dressing
- 1 cup salsa
- 1 tbsp dried oregano
- shredded Cheddar cheese, or more to taste
- 2 cups cooked rice, or to taste(optional)

Directions

- Cook beef and garlic over medium heat for about 7 minutes or until brown before adding corn, oregano, ranch dressing and salsa.
- Cook all this for 10 minutes.
- Pour this over rice for serving.

Serving: 4

Timing Information:

Preparation	Cooking	Total Time
10 mins	15 mins	25 mins

Nutritional Information:

Calories	815 kcal
Carbohydrates	50 g
Cholesterol	104 mg
Fat	56 g
Fiber	4.1 g
Protein	29.9 g
Sodium	1795 mg

* Percent Daily Values are based on a 2,000 calorie diet.

MEAT LOAF WITH OATS

Ingredients

- 1 lb ground beef
- 1 1/2 C. rolled oats
- 1 can French onion soup
- 2 eggs, beaten

Directions

- Set your oven to 375 degrees before doing anything else.
- Get a bowl, mix: beaten eggs, onion soup, oats, and beef.
- Put everything into your loaf pan.
- Bake for 1 hour and 20 mins. Ensure the internal temperature of the meat loaf 160 degrees before removing from oven.
- Enjoy.

Servings: 1 8-inch square pan

Timing Information:

Preparation	Cooking	Total Time
10 mins	1 hr	1 hr 10 mins

Nutritional Information:

Calories	265 kcal
Carbohydrates	18.1 g
Cholesterol	111 mg
Fat	12.9 g
Fiber	2.4 g
Protein	18.7 g
Sodium	496 mg

* Percent Daily Values are based on a 2,000 calorie diet.

SIMPLE PESTO

Ingredients

- 1/4 C. almonds
- 3 cloves garlic
- 1 1/2 C. fresh basil leaves
- 1/2 C. olive oil
- 1 pinch ground nutmeg
- salt and pepper to taste

Directions

- Set your oven to 450 degrees F before doing anything else.
- Arrange the almonds onto a cookie sheet and bake for about 10 minutes or till toasted slightly.
- In a food processor, add the toasted almonds and the remaining ingredients till a rough paste forms.

Amount per serving (6 total)

Timing Information:

Preparation	2 m
Cooking	10 m
Total Time	12 m

Nutritional Information:

Calories	199 kcal
Fat	21.1 g
Carbohydrates	2g
Protein	1.7 g
Cholesterol	0 mg
Sodium	389 mg

* Percent Daily Values are based on a 2,000 calorie diet.

Cheesy Artichoke Pesto

Ingredients

- 2 C. fresh basil leaves
- 2 tbsps crumbled feta cheese
- 1/4 C. freshly grated Parmesan cheese
- 1/4 C. pine nuts, toasted
- 1 artichoke heart, roughly chopped
- 2 tbsps chopped oil-packed sun-dried tomatoes
- 1/2 C. extra-virgin olive oil
- 1 pinch salt and black pepper to taste

Directions

- In a large food processor, add all the ingredients except the oil and seasoning and pulse till combined.
- While the motor is running slowly, add the oil and pulse till smooth.
- Season with salt and black pepper and serve.

Amount per serving (12 total)

Timing Information:

Preparation	
Cooking	5 m
Total Time	5 m

Nutritional Information:

Calories	118 kcal
Fat	11.9 g
Carbohydrates	1.1g
Protein	2 g
Cholesterol	3 mg
Sodium	92 mg

* Percent Daily Values are based on a 2,000 calorie diet.

American Pesto

Ingredients

- 4 C. packed fresh basil leaves
- 1/4 C. Italian parsley
- 2 cloves garlic, peeled and lightly crushed
- 1 C. pine nuts
- 1 1/2 C. shredded Parmigiano-Reggiano cheese
- 1 tbsp fresh lemon juice
- 1/2 C. extra-virgin olive oil, or more as needed
- salt and ground black pepper to taste

Directions

- In a food processor, add the parsley, basil, and garlic and pulse till chopped finely.
- Add the pine nuts and pulse till copped very finely as well.
- Add the cheese and pulse till combined.
- While the motor is running, slowly mix in the lemon juice.
- Then add the oil and pulse till well combined and smooth.

- Season with salt and black pepper and serve.

Amount per serving (6 total)

Timing Information:

Preparation	
Cooking	15 m
Total Time	15 m

Nutritional Information:

Calories	389 kcal
Fat	35.8 g
Carbohydrates	5.4g
Protein	14.1 g
Cholesterol	14 mg
Sodium	343 mg

* Percent Daily Values are based on a 2,000 calorie diet.

PASTA PESTO

Ingredients

- 4 C. fresh baby spinach
- 1/2 C. pecans
- 2 cloves garlic
- 1 C. Parmesan cheese
- 1 tbsp lemon juice
- 1/2 C. extra virgin olive oil
- 1 pinch salt and freshly ground black pepper to taste

Directions

- In a large food processor, add all the ingredients except the oil and pulse till combined.
- While the motor is running slowly, add the oil and pulse till well combined and smooth.

Amount per serving (16 total)

Timing Information:

Preparation	
Cooking	10 m
Total Time	10 m

Nutritional Information:

Calories	113 kcal
Fat	11.1 g
Carbohydrates	1.2g
Protein	2.5 g
Cholesterol	4 mg
Sodium	82 mg

* Percent Daily Values are based on a 2,000 calorie diet.

Asian Peanut Pesto

Ingredients

- 1 bunch cilantro
- 1/4 C. peanut butter
- 3 cloves garlic, diced
- 3 tbsps extra-virgin olive oil
- 2 tbsps diced fresh ginger
- 1 1/2 tbsps fish sauce
- 1 tbsp brown sugar
- 1/2 tsp cayenne pepper

Directions

- In a blender or food processor, add all the ingredients and pulse till smooth.

Amount per serving (10 total)

Timing Information:

Preparation	
Cooking	10 m
Total Time	10 m

Nutritional Information:

Calories	84 kcal
Fat	7.4 g
Carbohydrates	3.4g
Protein	1.9 g
Cholesterol	0 mg
Sodium	197 mg

* Percent Daily Values are based on a 2,000 calorie diet.

Pesto Spirals

Ingredients

- 1 tbsp olive oil
- 4 small zucchini, cut into noodle-shape strands
- 1/2 C. drained and rinsed canned garbanzo beans (chickpeas)
- 3 tbsps pesto, or to taste
- salt and ground black pepper to taste
- 2 tbsps shredded white Cheddar cheese, or to taste

Directions

- In a skillet, heat oil on medium heat.
- Stir in the zucchini and cook for about 5-10 minutes or till all the liquid is absorbed.
- Stir in the pesto and chickpeas and immediately reduce the heat to medium-low and cook for about 5 minutes or till the chickpeas and zucchini noodles are coated completely.
- Stir in the salt and black pepper and immediately place the zucchini mixture onto serving plates.

- Garnish the dish with the cheese and serve immediately.

Amount per serving (2 total)

Timing Information:

Preparation	10 m
Cooking	10 m
Total Time	20 m

Nutritional Information:

Calories	319 kcal
Fat	21.3 g
Carbohydrates	23.1g
Protein	12.1 g
Cholesterol	16 mg
Sodium	511 mg

* Percent Daily Values are based on a 2,000 calorie diet.

CLASSICAL BASIL CHICKEN

Ingredients

- 4 skinless, boneless chicken breast halves
- 1/2 C. prepared basil pesto, divided
- 4 thin slices prosciutto, or more if needed

Directions

- Coat a baking dish with oil then set your oven to 400 degrees before doing anything else.
- Top each piece of chicken with 2 tbsps of pesto then cover each one with a piece of prosciutto.
- Then lay everything into the dish.
- Cook everything in the oven for 30 mins until the chicken is fully done.
- Enjoy.

Amount per serving (4 total)

Timing Information:

Preparation	10 m
Cooking	25 m
Total Time	35 m

Nutritional Information:

Calories	312 kcal
Fat	19.3 g
Carbohydrates	2g
Protein	31.5 g
Cholesterol	83 mg
Sodium	434 mg

* Percent Daily Values are based on a 2,000 calorie diet.

Buffalo Fries

Ingredients

- cooking spray
- 4 large potatoes, sliced into wedges
- 2 tbsps olive oil, or to taste
- salt and ground black pepper to taste
- 1 C. Buffalo-style hot pepper sauce
- 1/4 C. melted butter, or to taste
- 1/4 C. ranch salad dressing, or to taste

Directions

- Coat a casserole dish with nonstick spray then set your oven to 400 degrees before doing anything else.
- Layer your potatoes into the dish and top them with some pepper, salt, and the olive oil.
- Cook the spuds in the oven for 35 mins then get a bowl and combine the melted butter and hot sauce.
- Stir the mix until it is smooth then add your potatoes to the mix.

- Stir everything to evenly coat the wedges then place the potatoes back into the dish.
- Top the potatoes with the ranch dressing.
- Enjoy.

Amount per serving (4 total)

Timing Information:

Preparation	10 m
Cooking	30 m
Total Time	40 m

Nutritional Information:

Calories	526 kcal
Fat	26.6 g
Carbohydrates	66.1g
Protein	8.1 g
Cholesterol	35 mg
Sodium	1765 mg

* Percent Daily Values are based on a 2,000 calorie diet.

Buffalo Spinach

Ingredients

- 5 oz. Pepper Jack cheese, shredded
- 1 (10 oz.) package frozen chopped spinach, thawed and drained
- 1/4 C. milk
- 1 tbsp sriracha

Directions

- Set your oven to 350 degrees before doing anything else.
- Get a casserole dish and add in: milk, spinach, and cheese.
- Stir the mix until it is smooth then cook it in the oven for 17 mins.
- Stir the mix twice as it cooks then add in your sriracha.
- Enjoy.

Amount per serving (8 total)

Timing Information:

Preparation	5 m
Cooking	20 m
Total Time	25 m

Nutritional Information:

Calories	84 kcal
Fat	6.1 g
Carbohydrates	2.5g
Protein	< 5.3 g
Cholesterol	20 mg
Sodium	137 mg

* Percent Daily Values are based on a 2,000 calorie diet.

Sriracha Chicken

Ingredients

- 4 skinless, boneless chicken breast halves
- 1 C. French salad dressing
- 1/4 C. salsa
- 1 tsp dried thyme
- 2 tbsps sriracha

Directions

- Coat a casserole dish with nonstick spray then set your oven to 350 degrees before doing anything else.
- Place your pieces of chicken in the dish then get a bowl and combine: thyme, dressing, and salsa.
- Top your meat with the dressing mix then place covering of foil over the dish.
- Cook everything in the oven for 25 mins then take off the covering and continue to cook the meat for 20 more mins.

- When 10 mins is left coat the chicken with the sriracha and continue cooking everything for 10 more mins.
- Enjoy.

Amount per serving (4 total)

Timing Information:

Preparation	10 m
Cooking	35 m
Total Time	45 m

Nutritional Information:

Calories	421 kcal
Fat	30.8 g
Carbohydrates	11g
Protein	25.3 g
Cholesterol	67 mg
Sodium	677 mg

* Percent Daily Values are based on a 2,000 calorie diet.

THANKS FOR READING! JOIN THE CLUB AND KEEP ON COOKING WITH 6 MORE COOKBOOKS....

http://bit.ly/1TdrStv

 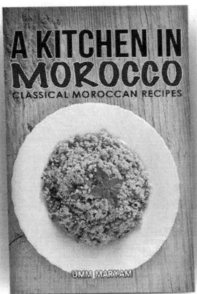 

To grab the box sets simply follow the link mentioned above, or tap one of book covers.

This will take you to a page where you can simply enter your email address and a PDF version of the box sets will be emailed to you.

Hope you are ready for some serious cooking!

http://bit.ly/1TdrStv

Come On...
Let's Be Friends :)

We adore our readers and love connecting with them socially.

Like BookSumo on Facebook and let's get social!

Facebook

And also check out the BookSumo Cooking Blog.

Food Lover Blog